H37/e

THE WINTER M

THE WINTER MAN

new poems by
Vernon Scannell

Allison & Busby
London

First published in 1973 by
Allison & Busby Limited, 6a Noel Street, London W1V 3RB

© 1973 Vernon Scannell

SBN 85031 101 2 (hardback)
SBN 85031 115 2 (paperback)

FOR JO

ACKNOWLEDGEMENTS are due to the British Broadcasting
Corporation and to the editors of the following journals:
*Cornhill Magazine, Encounter, The Listener, London
Magazine, New Statesman, Poetry Review, Stand,
Sunday Times, Transatlantic Review* and *Wave.*

*Printed in Great Britain by
The Anchor Press Ltd, and bound by
Wm. Brendon & Son Ltd, both of Tiptree, Essex*

Contents

Comeback

The wind is in a whipping mood tonight.
Whatever changes, these old noises don't.
My Grandad must have heard it much the same
And lain in bed and known that sleep had gone
To find a quieter place.

                  When I was twelve,
And that's a good half century ago,
I used to lie awake, not that the wind
Could scare sleep from my bed, but something could:
A sharp electric charge of restlessness
Would needle and excite for hours on end,
And, in imagination, I would touch
Each object of my shadow treasury—
An odd collection for a kid to love—
Not foreign stamps or hollow eggs in beds
Of cotton-wool, not model aeroplanes
Or rolling-stock, nor hoarded coins or cards,
But articles of apparatus, kit
And clothing of a special usefulness,
The paraphernalia of the fighter's craft.
It seems unlikely now that all that gear,
Which came to be the tackle and the tools
Of my life's trade, could thrill me in those days
As later only women's secrets could.
Yet that's the way it was, and even now
I catch a tiny tremor of the old
Excitement on the sagging wires of nerve
Recalling how I'd lay the objects out—
The black kid boots, white ankle-socks, the gloves
Like giant kidneys, skipping-rope and towel,

I

The glittering robe embroidered on the back
With my brave name; black satin trunks
With yellow stripes and wide band at the waist;
And no less sacred, no less magical,
The grim and necessary armour of
Gum-shield, jockstrap and protective cup.
Not that I really owned these things. Not then.
The only kit I had for training nights
Was my old sand-shoes, cotton football shorts
And winter vest. But one day I would wear
The finest stuff. I knew I'd make the big time,
And I did.

> *Listen to that wind.*
> *It's strange how all its anger comforts you,*
> *Maybe because it means I'm not alone;*
> *We share the long hours of the night, the two*
> *Of us, the old and tireless wind and me.*
> *Does the wind have memories to shuffle through?*
> *If so, they can't be very cheerful ones,*
> *Judging by that sound.*

> Oh, yes, I knew
I'd get to be a champion one day,
Though that was not the most important thing.
Important, yes, but what meant more to me
Was making myself good enough to wear
The garb the great ones wore. And even more
Important was the pleasure in the game,
Though "pleasure" seems too weak a word for that
Drench of power that filled you when you fought
And overcame with cunning, speed and skill
A tough opponent. Many times I've made
A perfect move, smooth as satin, quick as a cat,

The muscles thinking faster than a wink,
A double feint and counter, something you
Could never in a thousand lessons teach
An ordinary fighter to perform:
A miracle, a gift. Those moments make
Your life worthwhile.

                  The other stuff was muck:
I mean the silver trophies, medals, praise;
And later, fighting pro, the fancy belts,
The pictures on the sports page, interviews,
The youngsters scrambling for your scribbled name,
Even the big-time purses and the girls,
The bitches who would suck the virtue from you,
Press near your fame until the glitter dimmed,
They'd smear you with their artificial honey
And leave you spoiled and shamed.

                  I think it's strange
That when you've reached the top and won the crown
And every childish fantasy is fact,
It's strange how disappointing it all seems.
Success and fame, I've had the two and found
That both were fragile as those eggshell globes
They hang on Christmas trees. I used to think
The boys who'd never made the top, the ones
Who fought for peanuts in the shabby halls
And lost more often than they won, I thought
Them pitiable. Not now. They never knew
The failure of success, and they were real
Members of our craft, good workmen, proud
To wear the badges of the trade, a breed
That, if it dies, would surely mean the end
Of what I still believe the greatest game.

3

                              I won my first
Big title at the Albert Hall.
I fought a good old-timer from the North,
Birkenhead I think it was. He knew
The moves, was cagey as a monkey-house,
But he was past his best and in the seventh
I felt him weaken; as his strength seeped out
I seemed to suck it in like Dracula.
I put him down three times and in the ninth
He took a fast right-cross and folded up.
I knew he wouldn't rise. I did my dance
Above his fallen body, and the crowd
Bellowed their brainless worship of my feat.
I never thought that night my turn would come,
That eight years later in the selfsame ring
My nose would squash against the dust and resin
As I lay flat, I'd hear the same applause
But for the other man, new champion,
A youngster, strong, ambitious, arrogant.
By that time I had fought in Canada,
Twice at the Garden in New York, Berlin,
Milan and Paris, Rome, the Blackfriars Ring
And Stadium Club and places I've forgot.
I'd made and spent a fortune for those days,
And now they wrote me off. Another fool
Who once had been a fighter, now a ghost,
A fading name in yellowing papers, soon
Remembered only by a very few
And even they would get the details wrong
And, after too much booze, remember fights
I'd never had.

The wind is dying down
But still it makes its music, now less wild
But melancholy. It seems to sense my mood.
I doubt if I shall sleep tonight at all.
To tell the truth I have a taste for that
Sad sound of wind with darkness in its throat;
I like it when it snatches rain like seeds,
Throws handfuls at the window. But tonight
Is dry. No rain. No sleep. Only the wind
And memories.

After that defeat
I drank too much. I played the horses, too,
And lost the little capital I'd saved.
I was not old—a little over thirty—
Young enough in years, but I had fought
Two hundred contests as a pro, was tired.
But there was nothing else to do but fight.
It was my trade, the only one I knew.
And so I made my comeback, cut out booze,
Began to train with rope and heavy bag,
Run in the misty mornings through the park
And spar in the gym at night. I got a fight
In Leeds and put my man away in three.
I went back to the Club and showed them there
I still knew more about my business than
Those youngsters with their blasting energy
But little sense of what to do with it:
They sprayed their shots all round the field of fire;
I hoarded ammunition, only pressed
The trigger when I knew my shots would tell.
Once more my name appeared in fresh black ink,
My picture on a million breakfast tables.

They matched me for the title once again.
The fight was held in summer, out of doors,
White City was the place. The night was fine
And thousands came to see the veteran
Hand out a lesson to the cheeky boy
Who called himself the Champion. I knew
I'd win the title back. I'd seen him fight:
He was young and strong, with fair ability,
But I was master of a hundred tricks
He'd never heard about. I might be old
But I was also wise.

     The fight began
At nine o'clock at night as dark came down.
The arc-lamps gushed white brilliance on the ring.
Beyond the ropes, the crowd, a factory
Of noise and appetites, was idling now
Though very soon I knew the huge machine
Would roar to tumult, hammer out acclaim,
And I would be the target of that praise.
The comeback would succeed, though history
Was littered with the names of those who'd failed.
I would not fail.

     The first round proved to me
That my opponent was no better than
A score of fighters I had met before
And beaten easily. I jabbed and moved,
Slipping his leads and hurting him inside.
I took my time, collected points and foiled
His two attempts to trap me on the ropes.
The round was mine.

                The second round began
With brisker action from us both; he swung
A left and followed with an uppercut
Slung hard towards my heart. I moved away,
Stepped in and jabbed and jolted back his head;
I saw my chance and threw a big right hand.
I felt the jar to elbow as my fist
Connected with his jaw. He should have gone.
Most would. He staggered back but did not fall.
The engines of applause were roaring wild.
He faded back. I knew I had him then.
I took my time. I was too old a hand
To crowd in, throwing leather at his head.
I stalked him to the ropes and measured him:
A feint downstairs, a jab—I saw his chin
And threw again the punch to douse the lights—
I never knew what happened. Something burst
Inside my head; my skull was opened up
And starless midnight flooded into it.
I'll never know what happened on that night,
Why my right fist did not connect and end
The fight with me as Champion. They said
He beat me to the punch. Maybe. It seemed
A thunderbolt had fallen from the skies,
A biblical defeat, the fall of Pride.
One thing was sure: I had not won the bout
Nor would I ever have another chance.
I'd never be a champion again.

                I said that I'd retire,
Hang up the gloves for good, but very soon
I went into the ring, though now I knew
That I would never make the top again.

I fought in little halls and local baths,
Making a pound or two but taking some
Beatings from boys who five years earlier
Could not have laced my shoes. Sometimes I'd dream
That I would even yet surprise them all,
Come back and dazzle them with my old skill.
I nursed the dream till not so long ago
And then I gave myself a shake and said,
"Stop acting like a kid. You're grown up now."
I got a job as trainer at a club
In Bermondsey. It's fine. I like it there.
I taught those boys some things they'd never learn
From amateurs. I still work there. It's good.
I like to see them in the ring. I like
The smell of rubbing oils, to hear the swish
And slap of skipping-rope, the thud of fist
On bag. I like it all. I don't complain.
I'm quite a lucky man.

                                 The windows pale.
The wind itself seems tired now. I lie
Stretched out, but not to take the final count;
I have a round or two left in me yet.
My body is my own biography:
The scars, old fractures, ribs and nose, thick ear;
That's what I am, a score of ancient wounds
And in my head a few remembered scenes
And even those I'm not too sure about—
I've heard them say my brains are scrambled now—
I'm not too sure. Not sure of anything
Except I'm proud of what I've been—although
I would have liked another chance—sure, too,
I'll never make another comeback now
Unless the dead can make it, as some say.

Here and Human

In the warm room, cushioned by comfort,
Idle at fireside, shawled in lamplight,
I know the cold winter night, but only
As a far intimation, like a memory
Of a dead distress whose ghost has grown genial.

The disc, glossy black as a conjuror's hat,
Revolves. Music is unwound: woodwind,
Strings, a tenor voice singing in a tongue
I do not comprehend or have need to—
"The instrument of egoism mastered by art"—

For what I listen to is unequivocal:
A distillation of romantic love,
Passion outsoaring speech. I understand
And, understanding, I rejoice in my condition:
This sweet accident of being here and human.

Later, as I lie in the dark, the echoes
Recede, the blind cat of sleep purrs close
But does not curl. Beyond the window
The hill is hunched under his grey cape
Like a watchman. I cannot hear his breathing.

Silence is a starless sky on the ceiling
Till shock slashes, stillness is gashed
By a dazzle of noise chilling the air
Like lightning. It is an animal screech,
Raucous, clawing: surely the language of terror.

But I misread it, deceived. It is the sound
Of passionate love, a vixen's mating call.
It lingers hurtful, a stink in the ear,
But soon it begins to fade. I breathe deep,
Feeling the startled fur settle and smooth. Then I sleep.

The Discriminator

I can afford to discriminate
In the matter of female pulchritude,
Though I will readily admit
That, to many observers, my attitude
Must seem pernickety, even absurd.
This, of course, is not the way of it
Though I understand why the less fastidious
Call me poseur or hypocrite.
Take that girl over there—fine tits
I will concede, but her ankles are too thick.
Her eyes are pleasing, opalescent, dark
As a glass of stout held up to light,
But the mouth is so slack as to make you sick.
Her blonde companion, I must remark,
Is far too wide in the hips. She might
Be pretty enough, but in a style
So commonplace you must have seen
The same face in a hundred city streets.
I note your disbelieving smile.
Don't be deceived, young man; the time
Will come when you, too, will apply
The cool astringent judgement you observe
Me exercising now. Your eye
Will be, as mine, fastidious and cold,
And you will then display the fine
Wisdom and discernment of the old,
Enjoy the wages of experience,
Reject expediency and compromise
With the stern impartiality of age
And age's impotence.

The Defrauded Woman Speaks

The legend of my love and its defeat
Is soiled and crushed beneath indifferent feet.
Excrement and mud are smeared across
The words that cannot apprehend my loss.
I'm reckoned as pathetic or a joke,
Perhaps a bit of both. They say: "She's broke.
He's robbed her of her savings, every cent,
A cool twelve thousand, all the lot he spent
On other, younger women." And it's true.
I'm broke all right, and broken-hearted, too,
Though not because of all I had to spend
But just because the whole thing had to end.
I was not fooled, was always well aware
That he was lying, but I did not care.
The other women hurt, but what hurts more
Is that I'd never known such joy before
And never will again. You wonder why
I went into the box to testify
Against him. Vengeance maybe. I don't know.
One thing I'm absolutely sure of, though,
And this is it: I swear I'd gladly give
However many years I've left to live
For just another month with him; again
To hear his sweet deceitful whisper feign
A lovelier love than plain and honest fare;
To feel his hands exploring flesh and hair
Re-educating lust until it knew
How false such categories as false and true.

Jealous Lover

His head contains a room, a bed,
A dressing-table with open drawer
And shimmerfall of nylon, silk and lace.
Heels tap outside his ears.
The keyholes of his eyes are stuffed
With odourless jelly.
Panties flutter on the wishing-line.
A thieving finger stiffens in her purse.
He will learn Karate,
Disguised as a petrol pump
Stand white-faced in dark rain.
His stance is military, erect,
A thin Bunter, preposterous,
An auditor of drunken minstrelsy
Who has no home outside the myths
Of travellers who guffaw.
As midnight strikes all musics die.
The lights go out.
He is alone in bitter rain,
But, still erect, he throbs,
Alive
Until his crammed head bursts.

Confrontation

When we finally met, the hatred
That for weeks had been savoured
Was drained of taste;
We let it fall.
We looked at each other without fear,
With shyness and curiosity,
No loathing at all.

The impulse to smash bone and tear flesh
Was gone; no aftertaste
Lingered and sickened.
One did not forgive.
Forgiveness and blame were irrelevant
As knuckle-duster, cosh, revolver,
Or slick shiv.

My need was for the affection
I felt for him, and he
I am sure wanted mine.
Courteously we waited,
Uncertain, yet each with the knowledge
That through the bonds of her body
We were related.

I felt a rare generosity,
A kinship and sympathy;
Believed, in us both,
These might uncover
New areas of magnanimity
Dismissing such trivia as who
Was husband and who lover.

End of a Libertine

What kept him at the game
Was not
The obvious bait—
Delight in variety, the warm
Endorsement of his masculinity—
Nor did he need to compensate
For lack of mother-love.
No, danger was his favourite drink:
Though not an indiscriminate
And reckless boozer
Regular stiff shots for him
Had long become a strict necessity.

Those little potent risks,
The chance
Of being clawed
By furious fingernails; the threats
Of blackmail, suicide, unwanted son;
Fired on by a burst of tears,
Sniped at by malice, bored
To strangulation point by moans;
But things were not supposed to end
Like this—no rage
Of female eyes and nails,
But one bleak socket: the husband's hard black gun.

Love Nest

Perched high, it swayed when the wind was wild.
Roots were loosening in the stone.
It was not safe. Underground thunder
Rumbled, made it jerk and shudder.
He knew one day, or rather night,
The nest must fall: the place of loving
Was the place of death. He saw the picture:
Their fallen bodies on the ground,
Soldered together like a single creature,
Without a stitch or feather on,
For the world and his wife to look upon.

Gorgeous Girl

My element is danger; I walk taut threats.
The wind is shifty, wishes to undo me.
Snipers poke their muzzles over parapets,
All men are engines trembling to grunt through me.

I walk on wire; there are no safety-nets.
My beacon breasts capsized a thousand ships,
These haunches launched a quiver of huge rockets
Still orbiting the twin moons of my hips.

A buoyant billionaire of pulchritude
I must mistrust all men; they cannot love me.
"It's not your flesh I want," so many argued,
Eyes salivating as they loomed above me.

Most women would be glad to see me dead.
I hurry home and there take off my dress.
The mirrored beauty freezes in my head,
Hard ice, no kiss of glass can deliquesce.

Picture of the Bride

Alone, among the grey crosses and stones,
The slabs of marble, slippery as brawn,
Absolute as theirs the stillness she owns;
Her whiteness darkens the shades on the lawn.

Her features are hidden under the veil
Which also conceals the gleam of her hair;
Sepulchral she seems, not humanly frail,
Whiter and taller than any tomb there.

Sleeping Beauty

It was evening when he reached the place.
Outside, the air was motionless.
He listened for the sound of sigh or snore.
Silence trickled down his face;
He touched his sword for confidence,
Then parted the dark foliage at the door.

He entered. She was beautiful.
He pressed his mouth to hers; her lips
Grew warm and parted, breathing quick yet deep;
Her waking welcome magical,
Until her sharp teeth came to grips
And munched; for she was starved from that long sleep.

A Mystery at Euston

The train is still, releasing one loud sigh.
Doors swing and slam, porters importune.
The pigskin labelled luggage of the rich
Is piled on trolleys, rolled to waiting cars,
Grey citizens lug baggage to the place
Where fluttering kisses, craning welcomes wait.
A hoarse voice speaks from heaven, but not to her,
The girl whose luggage is a tartan grip
With broken zip, white face a tiny kite
Carried on the currents of the crowd.
The handsome stranger did not take her bag,
No talent-scout will ask her out to dine.
Her tights are laddered and her new shoes wince.
The Wimpy bar awaits, the single room,
The job as waitress, golden-knuckled ponce.
Whatever place she left—Glasgow, Leeds,
The village on the moors—there's no return.
Beyond the shelter of the station, rain
Veils the day and wavers at a gust,
Then settles to its absent-minded work
As if it has forgotten how to rest.

Miss Lonelyhearts Has Got It Wrong

Miss Lonelyhearts has got it wrong again.
She recommends as basis for a marriage
Shared interests; observes that even men,
Despite their bestial natures, will discourage
The placing of too great a value on
Those carnal pleasures that delight the savage.

Mere sexual excitement soon dies down;
The honeymoon is soon eclipsed, and after
Comes the testing time: transparent gown
Is swapped for decent flannel, and the laughter,
Kisses, music disappear upon
An anxious river banked by bricks and mortar.

Then, says Miss Lonelyhearts, you understand
How little physical attraction matters:
The gaze of firm respect, the friendly hand
Are far more precious than the tongue that flatters,
The squirm of limbs that parodies the damned.
She's just as wrong as in her other letters.

Or so it seems to me. Of course I know
That nothing mortal can endure forever,
But this lasts longer than the blinkered glow
Of mutual admiration or whatever
Miss L suggests will make a marriage go,
This hardening joy as loving time comes nearer.

The Widow's Complaint

You left as you so often left before,
Sneaking out on tiptoe,
No slam of door,
Off to drink with enemies of mine,
And of yours—
If you could only see it—
Drunkards and bores
Whose grossest flatteries
You swilled down with the booze
That you never had the gumption to refuse.
You won't come back this time.
No need to prepare
A welcome for you—clamped silence
And belligerent stare—
No need for morning nostrums or to hide
The whisky and car-keys,
Tighten my lips and thighs
Against your pleas,
No need for those old stratagems any more.
But you might have let me know what was in store;
Your last low trick
To leave me with no clue
That you had gone for good,
My last chance lost
To tell you what I've so long wanted to,
How much I hate you and I always have,
You pig, you bastard,
Stinking rat—
Oh, love, my love,
How can I forgive you that?

Five Domestic Interiors

i

The lady of the house is on her benders;
She's scrubbed and mopped until her knees are sore.
She rests a second as her husband enters,
Then says, "Look out! Don't walk on my clean floor."
He looks up at the slick flies on the ceiling
And shakes his head, and goes back through the door.

ii

She holds her chuckling baby to her bosom
And says, "My honey-pie, my sugar bun,
Does Mummy love her scrumptious little darling?
You're lovely, yes, you are, my precious one!"
But when the little perisher starts bawling
She says, "For God's sake listen to your son."

iii

Sandbagged by sleep at last the kids lie still.
The kitchen clock is nodding in warm air.
They spread the Sunday paper on the table
And each draws up a comfortable chair.
He turns the pages to the crossword puzzle,
Nonplussed they see a single large black square.

iv

The radio is playing dated music
With lilac tune and metronomic beat.
She smiles and says, "Remember that one, darling?
The way we used to foxtrot was a treat."
But they resist the momentary temptation
To resurrect slim dancers on glib feet.

V

In bed his tall enthusiastic member
Receives warm welcome, and a moist one too.
She whispers, "Do you love me? More than ever?"
And, panting, he replies, "Of course I do."
Then as she sighs and settles close for slumber
He thinks with mild surprise that it is true.

Song for a Winter Birth

Under the watchful lights
   A child was born;
From a mortal house of flesh
   Painfully torn.

And we, who later assembled
   To praise or peer,
Saw merely an infant boy
   Sleeping there.

Then he awoke and stretched
   Small arms wide
And for food or comfort
   Quavering cried.

A cry and attitude
   Rehearsing in small
The deathless death still haunting
   The Place of the Skull.

Outside, in the festive air,
   We lit cigars.
The night was nailed to the sky
   With hard bright stars.

Cold Spell

Take a black length of water,

                    leave it rippling as the day dies,

By morning it will be stretched taut,

                    pale and motionless, stiff silk.

Take a solitary puddle,

                    let it be nursed under sharp stars,

At dawn it will be a small blind mirror,

                    cold and milky.

The field in a single night

                    will age, grizzle and grow brittle;

Grasses will welcome destruction,

                    crunching underfoot.

Take a deep inhalation

                    and release slowly,

In the scentless air you will see

                    drifting bundles of breath.

Take a look at the sycamore and oak trees,

                    they will shame your softness

With their black calisthenics

                    gaunt against grey sky.

At sunset the dark cottage windows

                    will flush with a vinous infusion.

The furrows of mud in the field

                    might break a careless toe.

The cold spell works. Listen:

                    you can hear

The tap of hammers, the scrape of chisel,

                    the silver engines.

For disenchantment you must draw

                    fur and fire

Close, close to you, or better,
                                    embrace a live body,
Drink broth of warm breath,
                          eat each other.

Picnic on the Lawn

Their dresses were splashed on the green
Like big petals; polished spoons shone
And tinkered with cup and saucer.
Three women sat there together.

They were young, but no longer girls.
Above them the soft green applause
Of leaves acknowledged their laughter.
Their voices moved at a saunter.

Small children were playing nearby;
A swing hung from an apple tree
And there was a sand pit for digging.
Two of the picnicking women

Were mothers. The third was not.
She had once had a husband, but
He had gone to play the lover
With a new lead in a different theatre.

One of the mothers said, "Have you
Cherished a dream, a fantasy
You know is impossible; a childish
Longing to do something wildly

"Out of character? I'll tell you mine.
I would like to drive alone
In a powerful sports car, wearing
A headscarf and dark glasses, looking

"Sexy and mysterious and rich."
The second mother smiled: "I wish
I could ride through an autumn morning
On a chestnut mare, cool wind blowing

"The jet black hair I never had
Like smoke streaming from my head,
In summer swoop on a switchback sea
Surf-riding in a black bikini."

She then turned to the childless one:
"And you? You're free to make dreams true.
You have no need of fantasies
Like us domestic prisoners."

A pause, and then the answer came:
"I also have a hopeless dream:
Tea on the lawn in a sunny garden,
Listening to the voices of my children."

End of a Season

The nights are drawing in; the daylight dies
With more dispatch each evening;
Traffic draws lit beads
Across the bridge's abacus.
Below, black waters jitter in a breeze.
The air is not yet cold
But woven in its woof of various blues,
Whiffs of petrol and cremated flowers,
A cunning thread runs through,
A thin premonitory chill.
The parks are closed. Lights beckon from the bars.
The sporting news has put on heavier dress.
It is not autumn yet
Though summer will not fill
Attentive hearts again with its warm yes.

Far from the city, too, the dark surprises:
Oak and sycamore hunch
Under their loads of leaves;
Plump apples fall; the night devises
Frail webs to vein the sleek skin of the plums.
The scent of stars is cold.
The wheel-ruts stumble in the lane, are dry and hard.
Night is a nest for the unhatched cries of owls;
As deep mines clench their gold
Night locks up autumn's voices in
The vaults of silence. Hedges are still shawled
With traveller's joy; yet windows of the inn
Rehearse a winter welcome.
Though tomorrow may be fine
Soon it will yield to night's swift drawing in.

The athletes of light evenings hibernate;
Their whites are folded round
Green stains; the night
Reminds with its old merchandise—
Those summer remnants on its highest boughs—
That our late dancing days
Are doomed if not already under ground.
The playground gates are chained; the swings hang still,
The lovers have come down
From their deciduous hill;
Others may climb again, but they will not.
And yet the heart resumes its weightier burden
With small reluctance; fares
Towards Fall, and then beyond
To winter with whom none can fool or bargain.

Beside the Sea

Dark as braves, red as bricks from kilns
Or brown as loaves from ovens,
The faces of the veterans confirm
That the business of the sun had flourished
Before this diligent rain began.

And sun will hammer out its gold again,
Though when it does the gloom
Inside the heart and head will not disperse
Entirely: beneath the shimmering
Exuberance dark threads will creep,

Will drag against the flow, cold undertow,
While various boats put out
For trips across the bay, and on the beach
Little fists are fastened round
Olympic cones of frozen fire.

Sand will be slapped and deck-chairs fatten, groan,
As naked boys conceal
Their willies under prudently hung towels
And shops will flush with smooth pink rock
Seductive under cellophane.

But, as the sun presides and we applaud,
Dejection will persist,
A mist from off the sea, invisible,
Whose clinging weight will lie upon
The spirits like damp clouts.

Deny it as we might while daylight cries
With gulls and objurgations,
With noon's delight and shine,
At night we know, hearing its far, caged roar,
The greed and true vocation of the sea.

Incident at West Bay

He drove on to the quay.
His children, Mark and Jane,
Shrilled their needs:
A ride in a boat for Mark,
Ice-cream and the sands for Jane.

Gulls banked and glided over
The nudging dinghies; waves
Mildly admonished
The walls with small slaps.
It was the first day of the holidays.

"Wait there," he said, "I'll bring
Ice-cream." Out of the car
He felt the breeze
Easing the vehemence of the sun.
He said, "I won't be long."

He walked a few steps before
He was hit by a shout; he spun
Quickly round
To see his car begin
To move to the edge of the quay.

It was blind; it could not see.
It did not hesitate
But toppled in.
The sea was shocked, threw up
Astonished lace-cuffed waves.

He ran, he followed, plunged,
And in the shifting green gloom
He saw the car's
Tipped shape; he clutched handle, lugged.
His lungs bulged, punishing.

Through glass he saw their faces
Float, eyes wide as hunger,
Staring mouths,
Their lost and sightless hands.
In his chest the sea heaved

And pressed, swelled black and burst
Flooding his skull; it dragged
Him up to air.
They hauled him out and spread him
Oozing on the slimed stone.

They pumped the salt and darkness
From his lungs and skull;
Light scoured his eyes.
The sun said, "Rise." The gulls
Fell silent, then echoed his long torn yell.

Battlefields

Tonight in the pub I talked with Ernie Jones
Who served with the Somersets in Normandy,
And we remembered how our fathers told
The sad and muddy legends of their war,
And how, as youngsters, we would grin and say:
"The old man's on his favourite topic now,
He never tires of telling us the tale."
We are the old men now, our turn has come.
The names have changed—Tobruk and Alamein,
Arnhem, the Falaise Gap and Caen Canal
Displace the Dardanelles, Gallipoli,
Vimy Ridge, the Somme—but little else.
Our children do not want to hear about
The days when we were young and, sometimes, brave,
And who can blame them? Certainly not us.
We drank a last half pint and said goodnight.
And now, at home, the family is in bed,
The kitchen table littered with crashed planes;
A tank is tilted on its side, one track
Has been blown off; behind the butter-dish
Two Gunners kneel, whose gun has disappeared;
A Grenadier with busby and red coat
Mounts guard before a half a pound of cheese.
Some infantry with bayonets fixed begin
A slow advance towards the table edge.
Conscripted from another time and place
A wild Apache waves his tomahawk.
It's all a game. Upstairs, my youngest son
Roars like a little Stuka as he dives
Through dream, banks steep, then cuts his engine out,
Levels, re-enters the armistice of sleep.

War Cemetery, Ranville

A still parade of stone tablets,
White as aspirin under the bland
Wash of an August sky, they stand
In exact battalions, their shoulders square.

I move slowly along the lines
Like a visiting Commander
Noting each rank, name and number
And that a few are without names.

All have been efficiently drilled,
They do not blink or shift beneath
My inspection; they do not breathe
Or sway in the hot summer air.

The warmth is sick with too much scent
And thick as ointment. Flowers hurt,
Their sweetness fed by dirt,
Breathing in the dark earth underneath.

Outside the cemetery walls
The children play; their shouts are thrown
High in the air, burst and come down
In shrapnel softer than summer rain.

The Soldier's Dream

After the late shouts, the silences
Shattered like windows, rises
The bugle's husky hymn;
After the boozers' fumbled voices,
Their studs on stone, songs and curses,
The hard blokes are dumb.

After the last fag doused, small brightness
Crushed by the heel of darkness,
Lights out: the night commands.
After groans and expectorations,
Creakings like an old ship's timbers,
Sleep condescends.

In that consoling ambience
Images with unsoldierly elegance
Advance and are recognised.
After the day's gun-metal,
The khaki itch, such softness beckons,
Intentions undisguised.

Such challenge yet complete submission,
Small arms that need no ammunition
Beyond being feminine;
And other naked limbs, much longer,
Cancel parades, the day's loud anger,
With their own disciplines.

And after the cordite's lethal sweetness,
Reek of oil on steel, such fragrance,
A delicate silent tune;
And then the white thighs' open welcome,
The belly and breasts so suave and silken,
The moist dark between.

The bearded grin of generation
Calls the idler to attention,
Rouses the martial man,
Renews him as annihilator,
Restores his role, the man of leather,
Sinew, muscle, gun.

Muzzle flash and blast, bright blaring
Of the bugle of the morning,
The dream and darkness fled;
Orderlies of light discover
The soldier struggling with the lover
On the snarled, dishonoured bed.

Stanley's Dream

The village hall was changed: someone had moved
The church pews into it. There were many people there.
It was a summer evening, fragrant from
Anthologies of flowers. He could not see
All faces clearly, though one he saw quite plain:
Thomas Ashman, the carpenter from Trent.
But Thomas had been dead for eighteen months.
Or had he? Stanley was no longer sure.
Maybe he had dreamt that Thomas died,
For there was no mistaking that grained face,
And no one could deny he was alive
Since he was beckoning with urgent hand.
Stanley waved back and went across the room.
Then Thomas showed that he should bend his head
Close to his secret whisper. Stanley bent,
Then swiftly Thomas grabbed his neck and pulled
His startled face towards his own and pressed
His cheek to his old friend's, and Stanley felt
A coldness like a winter stone. The scent
Of flowers grew intolerably sweet,
The cold bit deep. He struggled to get free
And broke away from that embrace and from
The toils of sleep, but in his waking room
He felt the coldness burning on his cheek
And phantoms of dead flowers explored his throat.

Charnel House,
Rothwell Church

I remember the visit now,
See those tiers in the hall of my skull,
The little heads on shelves;
My nose remembers the smell,
Damp and chill, but not rank;
I remember the way they looked down,
Their eyes small, starless caves
In the grey and ochre and brown
Of skulls as cold as stones,
Looked down at the beautiful, neat
Composition of their stacked bones.
What a waste to gaol them away;
I would like some for my friends,
One to give to my wife
Next time I must make amends
For neglect or cruelty.
When I am away from home
It would not be any trouble,
It has no hair to comb.
And if she awoke to face it
Calm on her neighbour pillow
Where tenderly I'd place it
She'd welcome this better fellow,
The lack of fetid breath,
Know any words it could utter
Would have nothing to do with death.

Lives of the Poet

In Spring he saw the hedges splashed with blood;
Rags of flesh depended. In the moonlight
From a chestnut branch he saw suspended
A man who cocked an inattentive ear.
He heard worms salivate and paced his song
To the metronome of the hanging man,
Wore black to celebrate this time of year.

In August, from deceitful beaches, waves
Hauled drowners deeper in; he watched their arms
Wink in the obsolescent sun;
His ears discerned those other melodies
Beneath the chesty self-praise of the band,
The sound of blues. The shifting sand
And sea entombed clean bones, old summer days.

Now Autumn, vicar of all other weathers,
Performs its rites he joins the harvest chorus
At the cider-press and celebrates
In dance of words the seasons' grand alliance,
Puts on his snappiest suit on Friday nights
And stomps gay measures: no dirges now,
For Winter waits with ice and truth and silence.

A Dream of Books

Shadows were his escorts, echoes hid
In upper corners of the twilit room.
It was a library, but all the books
Were out of reach; the lowest shelf was feet
Above his head. The bindings of the books
Were uniform, untitled, anonymous
As spies or soldiers. A cold wind hurried through
The darkening room and rain was on its breath.
He longed to leave, but saw no way to go.
Like a shot bird, wings fluttering then still,
A single book fell at his feet; he knew
Between its covers every page was blank.
The wind began to cry and when he woke
His throat was thick with hurt, his face was wet.

Words and Monsters

When he was eight years old he had become
Hungry for words, and he would munch his way
Through comics, adverts, anything with some
Printed food to hold the pangs at bay.
His friends would hoard up birds'-eggs, shells or stamps,
But he collected words. One day he saw—
As he walked lonely down the town's main street—
A poster done in thunderous colours, raw
And red as flesh of newly butchered meat:
A picture of a lady, mouth distressed,
Eyes wild and fat with fear; and, underneath,
These glaring words: *THE ABYSMAL BRUTE—*
  The Best
Movie of the Year. He felt his teeth
Bite on the word *abysmal* as you test
The goodness of a coin. This one was fine.
He took it home to add it to the rest
Of his collection. He liked its shape and shine
But did not know its worth. Inside his head
Its echo rang. He asked his mother what
Abysmal meant. "Bottomless," she said.

The Abysmal Brute was grunting in the hot
Dark outside, would follow him to bed.

Legs

Of well-fed babies activate
Digestive juices, yet I'm no cannibal.
It is my metaphysical teeth that wait
Impatiently to prove those goodies edible.
The pink or creamy bonelessness, as soft
As dough or mashed potato, does not show
A hint of how each pair of limbs will grow.
Schoolboys' are badged with scabs and starred with scars,
Their sisters', in white ankle-socks, possess
No calves as yet. They will, and when they do
Another kind of hunger will distress
Quite painfully, but pleasurably too.
Those lovely double stalks of girls give me
So much delight: the brown expensive ones,
Like fine twin creatures of rare pedigree,
Seem independent of their owners, so
Much themselves are they. Even the plain
Or downright ugly, the veined and cruelly blotched
That look like marble badly stained, I've watched
With pity and revulsion, yet something more—
A wonder at the variousness of things
Which share a name: the podgy oatmeal knees
Beneath the kilt, the muscled double weapons above boots,
Eloquence of dancers', suffering of chars',
The wiry goatish, the long and smooth as milk—
The joy when these embrace like arms and cling!
O human legs, whose strangenesses I sing,
You more than please, though pleasure you have
    brought me,
And there are often times when you transport me.

Matters of Luck

When he lost the big one, a cut eye in the seventh,
A mean mouth over the left brow blabbing blood,
He fulminated for an hour, cursing his luck,
Chewing on rage and disappointment like the cud.

And over smaller things, too, the splinter he got
Chopping wood, the stubbed toe as he rose for a piss,
The punctured tyre on the way back from the dance,
The sore on his mouth repelling the mistletoe kiss.

His stinking luck, he said. And if more proof were needed
Any horse he backed would fall at the first fence;
The unexpected envelopes never contained cheques
But swollen bills and similar evidence.

He is practised in cursing. There are not many days
That pass without imprecations. And perhaps he is wise:
His oaths amulets against the real, withheld disasters—
The killers who play for keeps—a kind of praise.

Six Reasons for Drinking

"It relaxes me," he said,
Though no one seemed to hear.
He was relaxed: his head
Among fag-ends and spilt beer.
Free from all strain and care
With nonchalance he waved
Both feet in the pungent air.

ii

"I drink to forget."
But he remembers
Everything, the lot:
What hell war was,
Betrayal, lost
Causes best forgot.
The only thing he can't recall
Is how often before we've heard it all.

iii

"It gives me the confidence I lack,"
He confided with a grin
Slapping down ten new pennies
For a pint and a double gin.

iv

"It makes me witty fit to burst,"
He said from his sick-bed. "There's nothing worse
Than seeing a man tongue-tied by thirst.
Hey! Bring me a bed-pun quickly, nurse!"

From behind a fierce imperialistic stare
He said, "The reason's plain. Because it's there!"

vi

"It releases your inhibitions,
Let's you be free and gay!"
The constable told him brusquely
To put it away.

Drunk in Charge

We'd had a damned good party in the mess
The night before, went on a bit too long,
I wasn't feeling quite on form next day.
The Scotch I drank for breakfast didn't help.
I'd half a mind to go and see the quack
Except it wouldn't look too good, I mean
Going sick the morning of the big attack.
I soldiered on. I took a nip or two
While Grieves, my servant, laid my doings out.
An idle beggar, Grieves, but not too bad
As long as you administer the boot
From time to time. Certainly the chap's
Devoted to me, follow me to hell
And back he would. I thought I'd feel all right
After a decent shit, a bath and shave,
A breath of air, but nothing did much good:
Guts still complained, I couldn't see too well.
I took another nip before I mounted.
I rode out well enough and told my men
I knew they wouldn't let me down today—
Stout fellows, every one of them. We trotted off.
We heard the cannon of the enemy
Begin its din. We reached the starting line.
The bugle called. This was the time to show
My quality. I lit a long cheroot,
Pulled out my sabre like a long thin fish
And shouted, "Charge!" My damned cheroot went out.
"Hold on, my lads! Hold on!" I lit it up
And roared again through its blue fragrance, "Charge!"
My chestnut stumbled and it nearly fell.
I spurred him on but he reared up and tried

To throw me—a lesser rider would have gone.
I almost lost my long cheroot. I tried
To make him gallop but he wouldn't run.
Either he was lame or else a coward.
My squadron overtook me, thundered past,
Those gallant troopers, surging on towards
The wall of cannonade and musketry,
Hot for a glorious death or victory,
Fine fellows, splendid soldiers every one,
And not a smoke between the lot of 'em.

Not a Bad Life

I am my own hero and I worship me.
Often I loom at night outside the women's conveniences
And mumble through the bullets of my teeth.
When I spit, the leech of phlegm
Spawns a litter of condoms in the gutter.
I am not queer. I shall sleep
In bed soundly, deaf to the day's grum music
Which cannot disturb my repose.
When day slumbers
And the tolerant night gets up
I follow my customary employment:
I am a traveller
In ladies'
Undergrowth.
The commission is generous
And the wages are not derisory,
Could be called, I think,
A pretty good screw.

Confessional Poem

The impulse nags us all,
With some is clamorous;
The writing on the wall,
Though not, of course, by us,
Is proof, if proof were needed,
That few ignore the call.

We hear it loudest in
Double-beds and bars,
The order to begin
To show our wounds and scars,
Admit our little frailties,
Confess some venial sin.

Now I put down my own:
Extravagance and quaint
Lust when I'm alone
That, challenged, grows more faint;
I'm gullible, an easy
Touch for a trifling loan.

Yes, I admit each fault
As readily as you,
But shed no liquid salt
Though what I say is true,
For all are quite endearing—
You find that yours are, too?

Polling Day

Politics, said Bismarck, are not
An exact science. Neither is science,
At least it's not to me.
Towards each of these important matters
My attitude is less than reverential
Yet I accept that one cannot deny
The relevance of both, not now
Especially as I approach the booth,
Once more prepare myself
To make this positive, infrequent act
Of self-commitment, wishing that I could
Do more than scrawl a black anonymous mark—
The illiterate's signature
Or graphic kiss—against my favourite's name.
Incongruous, one thinks;
But is it so? In my case not entirely
Since I am voting unscientifically
For one who might be midwife to a dream
Of justice, charity and love
Or scatter obstinately truthful seeds
On these deceitful plots.
No argument or rhetoric could lend
My gesture and my hope more confidence,
So oddly apt this cross, illiterate kiss.

The Winter Man

Numb under the fresh fall
The stone of pavements did not feel
The blunted heel. Parked cars were furred
With ermine capes of recent snow;
Substantial silence showed both tint
And texture, bandaging the town
In lint of winter.

                    Looking down
From a window in a high warm room
A man recalled how, once before,
The slow hypnosis of the snow
Had veiled his senses in a trance,
How that pale dance composed its own
Spectral music and deceived—
When the sewing flakes had ceased—
With its white lie, a fraudulent
Paradigm of innocence.
And now, once more, the town wore white,
But he knew well the cold could kill,
That this bland lenitive possessed
No healing skill, would soon be soiled
And, like discarded dressings, show
The old wounds underneath, unhealed.
He did not trust the lying snow.

He turned away, sat by his fire,
A man of thirty-four, unsure
What stance to take, poised as he was
Precariously between the traps
Of youth and middle age; he feared

In equal parts the anguish of
Youthful passion and the absurd
Attitudes of ravenous love
Adopted by the man too old
To play the Prince with word and sword;
And yet he craved such exercise,
Yearned for the natural warmth it lent,
Half believed he could survive—
Without being too severely hurt—
Just one more non-decision bout.

He picked up his book but had not read
A page before the stillness jerked,
Pierced by a double jet of noise
Blurting through the silent room,
Official as a uniform.
The black shell raised, he said no more
Than half his name before a voice
Breathed close; he could have sworn he felt
The warmth of every whispered word.
She knew she did not have to say
Her name, less individual
Than that soft signature of sound.
He said: "It seems so long ago,"
And thought: How long? A year, or more?
Impossible to measure such
Desolation, so much hurt.
It seemed so long ago . . .

ii
Clock and calendar would both agree
That it was fourteen months ago when he,
Bored on a snivelling November night,

Stale as old crust, unable to read or write,
Called on some friends who would not aggravate
His subcutaneous itch, might mitigate
The threat of an enveloping despair.
When he arrived, at once he saw her there,
And all else in that room, human or
Inanimate, whatever dress it wore,
Was darkened and diminished by the claim
Her presence made, a solitary flame
Brilliant among spent ashes of the day.
Although the clock and calendar might say
That moment lifeless lay a year away
He reckoned otherwise: its essence stayed
Fixed in the heart, whatever else betrayed.
And other things remained to tantalize,
Awaken thwarted hungers and surprise
With half recaptured joys: a ride—
So trivial occasion to provide
A charge of such excitement and regret—
A ride in leather dusk when fingers met,
Uncertain for a second, then they clung
Miming longer limbs as if they'd flung
All clothing off; those moving hands amazed
With conscious nakedness and praised
Each other's strangeness and audacity.

Other minute events he could recall,
Gestures of lust and tenderness so small
No onlooker would know they had occurred.
And yet it was not long before he heard
A harsh inflection in her voice and she
Revealed impatience that could rapidly
Become contempt for all he seemed to be,

And had his reason not been on its knees
He would have known, however he might please
Her eyes and mind and flesh on friendly days,
He never could possess her and must face
The truth that her desire was spiked with hate.
So when, as winter laid down arms to spring,
The season when, in fiction, everything
In nature welcomes lusty grooms and brides
But is, in fact, peak time for suicides,
He realised, once the first raw pain had eased,
Like a man informed he's mortally diseased,
Her words confirmed what he had always known:
In spring she turned indifferent as stone
And told him that the time had struck to go,
Her winter love had melted with the snow.

For days he dozed, bemused, and then began
The ache that trailed him like a Private Eye
To cafés, bars, surprising him with sly
Disguises in the street or public park,
Tapping his line, transmitting in the dark
Messages whose sense he could not quite
Seize before each cypher slipped from sight.
He found, again, he could not read or write.
Down avenues of summer lovers walked;
The green tongues in the trees above them talked
A language that endorsed their bodies' speech,
Yet with the sun's connivance could not reach
Those icy fetters clamped on feeling's source.
And when sun paled with Autumn's sick remorse
And leaves swam in the morning milk of air
As smoke from garden bonfires rose like prayer,
He was unmoved; until fresh winterfall

Prepared white silence to sustain that call
Thrilling the waiting stillness of his room,
A double blade that stabbed with hope and doom.

iii

He said, "It seems so long ago,"
And waited, holding to his ear
The black shell in which low susurrus
Rose and fell, a dream of surf.
He would not go.
Yet even as intention shaped
He felt it melt, a single flake
Of snow that settles on warm stone.
Slowly he lowered the telephone,
Found his coat, switched off the lights
And went down to the white, stunned street.
The coldness glittered in his eyes.
Beneath the stroking wind the fur
Of snow was riffled, then smoothed down.
The stars were frozen chips of flint.
The flesh grew warm, his eyes were bright.
Anticipation drummed and strummed;
Uncertainty sniped at his heart,
Premonitory fear was sharp
And lingered on the tongue, although
A sweeter taste was there also,
Wafer of hope, a desperate joy.
His footprints trailed him through the snow.